TO THE CHURCH AT THESSALONICA

GIFMA INC founded By Dr. Nich Mbaezue MPA/PhD is headquartered in Richmond, Texas and is devoted to the preaching of Jesus Christ and service to humanity worldwide.

Copyright © GIFMA INC

All rights reserved. No part of this publication may be reproduced, stored in a retrieval system, or transmitted, in any form or by any means, electronic, mechanical, photocopying, recording, or otherwise, without the prior permission of GIFMA INC.

All Editing and Publishing courtesy of:

BLACK BOX PUBLICATIONS

ATLANTA, GA

CONTENTS

Introduction 1

Background 6

PART - ONE 19

   Chapter - 01 20

   Chapter - 02 38

   Chapter - 03 55

   Chapter - 04 69

   Chapter - 05 84

PART - TWO 108

   Chapter - 01 111

   Chapter - 02 121

   Chapter - 03 133

INTRODUCTION

The book of Thessalonians is unique in terms of its timing, the circumstances it addressed, and its richness in basic doctrinal teaching.

First, its timing. This was the letter Paul to the very first church he founded. He had exited Thessalonica under some very unpleasant circumstances and was penning this letter from his new location at Corinth. It was the custom of Paul and his team to arrive a place, preach the gospel, win converts, disciple them, establish a church there and appoint a leader for them, and gladly move on. In this case they left before their normal term could be over. A minister was hurriedly raised from amongst the young disciples and charged with the new role of pastoring the flock, whilst the apostolic team moved on.

TO THE CHURCH AT THESSALONICA

Because transportation between cities was very laborious in those days, and telephones didn't exist, the only convenient means of exercising Paul's role of overseer to the Church was by sending letters via a human courier.

> *The epistles were delivered by hand and read publicly, not only at thessalonica, but also at the churches in neighboring towns and cities.*

We see this in 1 thessalonians 5:27:

> *I charge you by the Lord that this [a]epistle be read to all the holy brethren.*

and Col 4:16:

Now when this epistle is read among you, see that it is read also in the church of the Laodiceans, and that you likewise read the epistle from Laodicea.

These epistles served as the final authority on all and every matter in dispute, as they conveyed Paul's final verdict on the matter, whatever it be. 2 Thess 3:14:

> *And if anyone does not obey our word in this [a]epistle, note that person and do not keep company with him, that he may be ashamed.*

The timing of this epistle 54 AD was just a few years after the Resurrection of the Lord and the coming of the Holy Spirit at Pentecost. The Church had come under fierce persecution at Jerusalem and were forced to disperse to the nearby cities of the Gentiles. That the Thessalonian church got established and thrived amid great persecution is an eloquent testimony of her resilience, being the only notable church outside of Jerusalem and also mostly populated by Gentiles.

The second aspect of its uniqueness is with regards to its richness in doctrine and the fundamental truths. The purpose of all scripture is to establish doctrine, to reprove and correct wrongdoing, and for general instruction in righteousness.

> [6]*Take heed to yourself and to the doctrine. Continue in them, for in doing this you will save both yourself and those who hear you.*
>
> **2 Tim 4:16:**

The foundation of it all is doctrine. The epistle to the Thessalonians was skewed more towards doctrine than any other area. For this reason, it marks a good beginning for new disciples, starting them off on the right track, whilst also serving to strengthen and comfort those already long in the faith, when it is properly taught and espoused. In the case of the Thessalonian church, Paul's epistle helped transform them into an outstanding testimony to other churches round about, just in as few as two years. They demonstrated God's power as evidence of the entrance of the gospel. To Paul, they were an eloquent testimony and a handsome reward for all his labor in the gospel.

TO THE CHURCH AT THESSALONICA

BACKGROUND

Acts 17:1

"Now when they had passed through Amphipolis and Apollonia, they came to Thessalonica, where was a synagogue of the Jews: And Paul, as his manner was, went in unto them, and three sabbath days resesoned with them out of the scriptures: opining and alleging, that Christ must needs have suffered, and risen again from the dead; and that this Jesus, whom I preach unto you, is Christ.

While some of them believed, and consorted with Paul and Silas; especially of the devout Greeks a *great multitude, and of the chief women not a few, the Jews which believed not, moved with envy, took unto them certain lewd fellows of the baser sort, and gathered a company, and set all the city on an uproar, and assaulted the house of Jason, and sought to bring them out to the people.*

And when they found them not, they drew Jason and certain brethren unto the rulers of the city, crying, 'These that have turned the world upside down are come hither also, whom Jason hath received: and these all do contrary to the decrees of Caesar, saying that there is another king, one Jesus.

And they troubled the people and the rulers of the city, when they heard

> *these things. And when they had taken security of Jason, and of the other, they let them go.*
>
> *And the brethren immediately sent away Paul and Silas by night unto Berea: who coming thither went into the synagogue of the Jews".*

Thessalonica was the capital and largest city of the Roman province of Macedonia. The presence of an important highway in this city which connects Rome to the Oriental region, as well as a large seaport made Macedonia one of the wealthiest and most flourishing centers in Greece. It earned recognition from the Central Roman Authority as a free city and was accorded self-rule.

There were many Jews in the city and a prominent synagogue of the Jews. Due to the cosmopolitan nature of Thessalonica, it had many pagan religions and cultural influences that challenged the Christian faith. Yet, Paul judged Thessalonica a very strategic place to plant the gospel taking advantage of that.

Upon arriving Thessalonica, he followed his typical approach which was to enter the synagogue and confront the Jews with the gospel of the Christ Jesus. Every genuine effort at planting the gospel must have an element of characteristic boldness. You cannot free people from decades or even centuries of lock-down by wrong religion, without confronting their doctrines head-on. Indoctrination is a very strong element in every religion and a person hooked on wrong doctrine, requires the grace of God to liberate. It is worse when this wrong doctrine has been handed down over generations. Someone said, and I agree, that when falsehood I institutionalized over a long period of time, any speaking of truth is viewed as rebellion.

The Law of Moses was such. The Jews esteemed Moses very highly and his laws were held sacrosanct. Unlike the Jews who were well drunk with the old wine of the Law, the Gentiles of Thessalonica were free from such religious addictions, and therefore presented a virile, willing and ready platform for the gospel.

Latching unto that advantage, Paul brutally assaulted the traditions and beliefs of the Jews by openly alleging and arguing from the same Torah they held so highly and read all their lives, that Jesus Christ is truly their awaited Messiah.

You will also notice as you get very familiar with the New testament that neither Paul, nor Peter, John, James or Jude, the major writers of the New Testament epistles tried to quote from the teachings of Christ. Instead they reasoned from the old testament scriptures, the Law and the Prophets. They took scriptures from the Books of Moses to confirm their message of the gospel of Christ.

The reason for this deliberate blank-out of Christ's teachings was two-fold. First, Christ taught from the Law of Moses and his teachings were directed to the Jews who were under the Law, so that He (Christ) could fulfill the Law. This was his mission on earth. It wasn't meant for the Gentiles, who were free from the Law of Moses.

Gal 4:4-5

But when the fulness of the time was come, God sent forth his Son, made of a woman, made under the law,

To redeem them that were under the law, that we might receive the adoption of sons.

Secondly, the preaching of Jesus Christ was a strange doctrine to the Jews who were the dominant God's tribe of that time. Quoting from Christ who they considered an 'impostor' would have been counterproductive. Besides, the epistles were New Testament teachings directed at the Church (both Jews and Gentiles) which is the pillar and ground of Truth.

Paul was never the man who to shy away from confronting wrong doctrine when and where necessary. So, he did the needful by openly asserting from scriptures that Christ need have suffered. That Christ need have risen from the dead. And that this Jesus whom he preached was indeed the Christ, the awaited savior of the world.

Acts 17:2-3.

² As was his custom, Paul went into the synagogue, and on three Sabbath days he reasoned with them from the Scriptures, ³ explaining and proving that the Messiah had to suffer and rise from the dead. "This Jesus I am proclaiming to you is the Messiah," he said.

Doctrinal sanctity is so important in the preaching and teaching of the gospel. This is one thing so glaringly lacking in the content and context of the charismatic gospel movement of our day. As a result, it has been difficult to truly espouse the gospel to the multitudes of converts.

The orthodox Christian groups made sure their doctrines, essentially a mixture of Law and Grace, were well engrained in their adherents. Indoctrination of their followership was complete and total, and hence, any effort to teach them something new; or to espouse them to the true gospel of grace must be un-apologetically sharp in contrast, rich in pure doctrine and presented in a direct and sincere engagement with the hearer. This is not presently the case with the charismatics, especially the Pentecostals.

For instance, only in a Pentecostal Church could someone take up a microphone and relate a so-called 'dream' or 'vision' of having traveled to Heaven or Hell, met with God or Satan and returned to earth, with so many tales that do not line up with the Scriptures or the New Testament. Surprisingly, you will find many sitting and gulping all that ignorant stuff. Some are even moved to give offerings to such people.

Again, among the Charismatics groups of today, people come to Church with all manner of materials to 'collect anointing'- as they call it. Sometimes the list of items includes bottles of oil, handkerchiefs, and even cutlasses and whips to be used afterwards to battle down the Devil.

Paul and other New Testament writers warned believers to abhor such.

1 Tim 1:3

"As I urged you when I went into Macedonia, stay there in Ephesus so that you may command certain

people not to teach false doctrines any longer".

Eph 4:14

"Then, we will no longer be infants, tossed back and forth by the waves, and blown here and there by every wind of teaching and by the cunning and craftiness of people in their deceitful scheming".

2 John 2:10

" If anyone comes to you and does not bring this doctrine of Christ, do not take them into your house or welcome them."

TO THE CHURCH AT THESSALONICA

In Thessalonica, Paul did exactly that. He taught the pure doctrines of grace of God in Christ Jesus which included in the main:

1. The need for the Jews to turn completely away from the Law of Moses and from the Prophets to embrace the New doctrine of the risen Christ.

2. That the Gentiles turn away from idols to Christ Jesus.

3. That Jesus is God manifest in the flesh and indeed the Christ. And that through his death, burial and resurrection, salvation hath come to all men, both Jews and Gentiles alike.

4. That Jesus Christ is coming back to earth again in glory.

5. That all who believe in Christ and receive him are instantly justified; and have a sacred hope of being delivered from the wrath of God that will come upon the world when Christ appears in glory.

6. That all saints, those who died in Christ, and those who are alive shall at some future date be caught up in the air with the Lord and shall be exempted from the terrible happenings preceding His return.

7. That Christians need not sorrow over their loved ones who die in Christ, because their souls are not lost, but rather they have gone to be with the Lord pending when all believers shall be united again.

Paul's strong defense of the gospel was greeted with mixed responses. Some believed. A great multitude of devout Greeks cast their lots with Paul's argument especially the noble women and members of the upper class of the Greek society. But the Jews whose doctrines and traditions were under assault by Paul, and whose ego got bruised in the process stirred up an uproar, expelling Paul and Silas from their city.

TO THE CHURCH AT THESSALONICA

This countermove by the Jews came a bit too late though, as the Church of Thessalonica was already birthed. ALLELUIA!

Part - One

TO THE CHURCH AT THESSALONICA

CHAPTER - 01

1.1

"Paul, and Silvanus, and Timotheus, unto the church of the Thessalonians which is in God the Father and in the Lord Jesus Christ: Grace be unto you, and peace, from God our Father, and the Lord Jesus Christ".

Paul, Silas and Timothy here send their greetings to the disciples at Thessalonica, reminding them that they were privileged to be in God the Father and in the Lord Jesus Christ. This is a clear proof that the two members of the Godhead are distinct personalities.

Curiously in this epistle, Paul refrained from addressing himself by the title 'Apostle of Jesus Christ' or 'Servant of God' which he often used in his letters. The Thessalonian Church was different. He was so intimate with this group, being his first work in church planting. Many church-planters and pioneer evangelists will readily agree that such lofty introduction was unnecessary. You easily become inseparable from your first converts to faith and those with whom you labored in the planting of a Church. Paul was held in very high esteem and affection by this Church that he had no need to assert Apostolic authority in his epistle.

'Grace and Peace' he prayed upon them. You couldn't confer any greater blessing upon a believer than the grace of our Lord and the peace of Christ that transcends whatsoever the world could give. John 14:27.

TO THE CHURCH AT THESSALONICA

1.2

"We give thanks to God always for you all, making mention of you in our prayers".

A Church never really outgrows the need for prayers as it will most assuredly come under constant attack and buffeting by Satan. Paul, as all shepherds ought to do often, never ceased to pray for every Church he planted. He prayed for the Philippian Church (Phil 1:3-4), and the Colossians (Col 3:1). The Church especially a young one requires prayers, just like any infant needs milk. Under the New Testament prayer however should never boil down to begging God to preserve the Church or to prosper it. No. It is already His express will. Prayer for the Church should serve as our opportunity or means of enforcing that will.

Christ himself already declared: "I will build my Church, and the gates of Hell cannot prevail against it".

When we pray, it is to re-enforce our status and understanding of our victory over all opposing forces because of Christ's finished work.

1.3

"Remembering without ceasing your work of faith, and labor of love, and patience of hope in our Lord Jesus Christ, in the sight of God and our Father";

Here the Apostle rehearses his memory of the Thessalonian saints as of a healthy Church.

First, he remembers their work of faith. These believers had a sincere, active and productive faith, devoid of pretenses and lip service, and backed up by a depth of commitment. For many born-again Christians today, their commitment goes no farther than responding to an 'altar call' and praying the sinner's prayer'. Next is they become seekers of signs and wonders: healing, miracle, spouse, job, travel visa, things, things and things...

But Jesus Christ did not die so we can have things. Things He said will follow us naturally if we seek him and his Kingdom. Seeking the Kingdom means submission to the Lordship of Christ is every way. Turning roundabout from 'works' righteousness to Grace and true holiness. This only comes through faith in the blood of Christ and the washing of water by the Word.

Titus 3:5:

5 ——— *not by works of righteousness which we have done, but according to His mercy He saved us, through the washing of regeneration and renewing of the Holy Spirit,*

The Thessalonian Church labored in love for one another. Faith works through love, sincere love for one another which Paul commended.

Another striking virtue of the Thessalonian Church was their 'patient hope'. A hope placed where it rightly belonged, not on Paul but upon Christ. Not on any Bishop or Prophet, but upon the Lord.

Today, many profess to be believers, but in actual sense their faith and allegiance is to their 'man-of-God' rather than to Christ. When you hear them say "my God never fails", what is meant is that God will never fail so-so- and- so TV Evangelist, or Bishop, or General Overseer of their denomination. They have no trust placed upon the Lord, but rather upon a man as an intermediary, because in their estimation they could never measure up to God's standards, let alone intcract with him.

'Patient hope in the Lord Jesus Christ' is the true benefit of faith. Faith is the currency whilst hope is the goods purchased by faith. They that trust in their God shall not make haste. (Isaiah 28:16).

Hope is defined by how we wait, not just how long. Hope means we wait in patient and quiet confidence, that he who promised is able to do it. Prophet Isaiah put it differently saying: For thou shalt cause him to dwell in perfect peace, he whose mind is stayed upon thee. (Isaiah 26:3)

1.4

"Knowing, brethren beloved, your election of God."

The ultimate of all faith in Christ is to come to the full knowledge of the 'election of grace'. You barely know God until you know 'His election'. You are elect means you're saved by grace and therefore have no role or input into it except to receive.

Ephesians 2:8

8 For by grace you have been saved through faith, and that not of yourselves; it is the gift of God,

Yea, it was God who chose you for Himself and not the other way around, and His gifts and calling are without repentance. He is able and willing to save to the uttermost those who come to Him and the life he gives is eternal. There's something about this knowledge of Christ's love that passes all understanding and fills us with the fullness of God.

1.5

> *"For our gospel came not unto you in word only, but also in power, and in the Holy Ghost, and in much assurance; as ye know what manner of men we were among you for your sake".*

The message content of a preaching is important, but what is more important is the manner of delivery, the relationship setting or what the Bible calls your "conversation" among your hearers.

Here Paul highlights the importance of the presence of the HolyGhost in that interaction, as well as the personal relational conduct of the minister.

Paul's ministry scored high marks in all these attributes and hence the outstanding results at Thessalonica in as short as three years. The

Thessalonians stood firm amid persecution, buoyed by Paul's example.

Paul's ministry came to them 'in word', 'in power', and 'in the HolyGhost'; and 'with much assurance'. That ought to be the standard modus of delivering the gospel. There are four key components to it:

- **"In word"** – Paul preached the Word of God, not fables or genealogies. A young Church needs the sincere milk of the Word to grow, and an already thriving Church requires "strong meat" to stay healthy and strong. Anything short of this is an abuse and malnourishment, which will not only lead to a stunted spiritual growth, but also a vulnerability to Satanic attacks.

Colossians 2:6-7

⁶As you therefore have received Christ Jesus the Lord, so walk in Him, ⁷rooted and built up in Him and established in the faith, as you have been taught, abounding ⁽ᵃ⁾in it with thanksgiving.

➲ **"In power"** – Power in this context refers not so much to signs and wonders although this was very present in his gospel, but rather to the power of the joyful effect of the 'too-good-to-be-true' news of grace. The gospel is good news. News of the extravagant grace of God which he has lavished upon all men. When it is received and obeyed, lives are changed; and destinies of persons, families and even cities are transported to greater heights. That was the case of Samaria when they received the gospel preached by Phillip. The good news should be delivered with power and conviction. The gospel is more than a mere collection of interesting facts and stories. It is the power of God unto salvation to anyone who believes.

We need to take stock periodically by asking ourselves the pertinent question:

"What effect has the new birth had in my life since I believed"?

Unfortunately, for some the answer will be little or nothing. There be some believers that if they got arrested and charged to a court of law for their faith in Christ, there will be 'no evidence' to convict them. The HolySpirit changes people when they believe the gospel. We are to expect these changes, but at the same time we should be patient to see them manifest in our lives and in the lives of our fellows. God's power not our cleverness or persuasive ability is what gets the job done in our hearers.

- "With the HolyGhost" – This points to the actual doer of the gospel work, the Spirit of God himself. No man can yield to the gospel or confess Jesus Christ as lord except by the HolyGhost.

- Without his own role in the work, our words are powerless to the unconverted. The HolyGhost convicts the world of sin and at the same time assures the saved of their eternal life. Both roles are very vital and pivotal for a healthy Church.

- The HolyGhost also brings revelation. Revelation is the oxygen of faith. A drab spiritual atmosphere is created wherever the Word is taught without revelation and received with mental assent only. Such spirituality can only endure for a while. (See Mark 4:15-17- parable of the sower)

- "With much assurance" – refers to the re-assuring conduct of the minister. Paul's ministry was very relational to the Thessalonians. "Ye know what manner of life we lived among you for your sakes" he says. That means it was a deliberate effort by Paul and his colleagues to model Christlikeness to the young Church, and to make the gospel so endearing, through their personal conduct. The Thessalonians were persuaded of the truth of the gospel because Paul, Silas and Timothy lived it. Every minister of the gospel and indeed every believer should ask: "Does my life confirm or contradict the gospel?

The personal conduct of a believer is important, especially those who aspire (and every one of us should) to leadership. It is for that reason that Paul wrote to Timothy and Titus in later epistles stipulating the qualifications of Deacons, Elders,

Bishops and even Widows. (See Titus 1:7, 1Tim 3:2)

1.6

"And ye became followers of us, and of the Lord, having received the word in much affliction, with joy of the Holy Ghost."

In any place where you have a Spirit-filled exposition of the gospel, conversion and followership is only natural. The gospel is good news which draws adherents wherever it is communicated in simple and sincere terms. The Thessalonians received the gospel with immense joy but were immediately faced with fierce persecution from both the Jews and own countrymen. Here in this epistle, Paul acknowledges that. Especially, the fact that they still retained their joy in the HolyGhost despite afflictions. The joy of the Lord should be an all-time antidote to fear, dismay and disillusionment when facing persecution for the gospel. You cannot respond to persecution with joy if the joy of the HolyGhost is not already bubbling in your inside. The source of it being the knowledge of the truth of God's grace, and bonded fellowship with the brethren. Born-again does not preclude persecution and trials. Fear not them who are only able to destroy the body Jesus said.

After they received Christ, the Thessalonians apparently weren't exempted from death until the return of the Lord. No. Howbeit, when believers were persecuted even to death, some questioned their faith and began to draw back. A greater part of this epistle was used by Paul to address this issue and encourage them, explaining what happens when a believer 'sleeps in the Lord'.

TO THE CHURCH AT THESSALONICA

1.7

"So that ye were ensamples to all that believe in Macedonia and Achaia".

The Thessalonian Church became a shining example to all other Churches within the region. Our conduct in faith is more important in terms of how it impacts upon others. For as a piece of iron sharpens another piece, so a man is sharpened by the conduct of another. (Proverbs 27:17).

The fervency of spirit in a believer, or a Church is often contagious. The Word of God and the testimony of Christ began to ring out from Thessalonica to people everywhere even beyond Greece. Paul attests that wherever he went to preach, people received him with open arms because of the testimonies from Thessalonica.

Sometimes our reputation as preachers precedes us. Such that we needn't have opened our mouths to preach to someone before they have noticed there's something peculiar about us. It is that difference and peculiarity that does the speaking more, even to critics and adversaries of the gospel. The Bible says that whilst they falsely accuse you of wrongdoing, beholding your personal conduct, they will be shamed in their conscience. (1 Peter 3:16)

TO THE CHURCH AT THESSALONICA

CHAPTER - 02

Paul goes a step to refresh the Thessalonians of the manner of interaction he and his colleagues had with them. These could readily serve as guidelines for Pastors and Church planters of all ages.

2.1-2

"For yourselves, brethren, know our entrance unto you, that it was not in vain:

²But even after that we had suffered before, and were shamefully entreated, as ye know, at Philippi, we were bold in our God to speak unto you the gospel of God with much contention".

First, he reminds them that their joint effort bore good fruits, it was not in vain. Having escaped from maltreatment in Phillipi, Paul and his team arrived Thessalonica to face an even more stout opposition and a harsher persecution. They remained undaunted and alas, the Church birthed in Thessalonica served them for a trophy.

Fear of imprisonment or even death should not deter any spirited bearer of the gospel from preaching it, for the Lord is backing us up all the way. Sometimes it may not be an obvious persecution. It could be as subtle as rejection from friends and family, career associates, and even some brethren or fellow Church members.

2.3

"For our exhortation was not of deceit, nor of uncleanness, nor in guile:"

You yourself can see we were not preaching with any impure purposes, deceit or trickery. This statement must have come as a rebuttal of some false allegations levelled against Paul by his adversaries in-order to cause dis-affection amongst his followers. This tactic still being used commonly aims at discrediting genuine gospel teaching with the tag of "cheap grace". Philippians 3:18.

Paul defended himself by reminding them of his conduct amongst them. He did not seek money, fame or popularity to which they could all bear witness. It is important that ministers harbor the purest of motives to be able to give this kind of Paul's defense when the need arises.

2.4

"But as we were allowed of God to be put in trust with the gospel, even so

we speak; not as pleasing men, but God, which trieth our hearts."

We are only messengers who have been entrusted by God with the gospel and we cannot but speak as such. The first duty of a genuine gospel bearer is to realize that it is 'a position of trust'. Trust given by no less a person than the Lord himself shouldn't be a thing to trifle with. Even though God will not strike you dead as in the Old testament, there are still grave consequences for this. Corrupt communication, guile, and men pleasing talks are some of the subtle ways the Enemy will tempt us to trifle with the gospel. Paul says the if we seek to please men by telling them what they want to hear or by judging fleshly judgements, we cannot be the servants of Christ. Gal 1:10

Paul never changed or diluted the gospel to make it more acceptable to an audience. The methods of communicating it may vary, but the contents and doctrine remains constant. The truth of the gospel which is the 'finished work' of Christ and unconditional eternal life of the redeemed must not be compromised.

2.5

"For neither at any time used we flattering words, as ye know, nor a cloak of covetousness; God is witness".

Our methods must exclude every form of guile, jesting or willful display of oratorical skills. Flattery is often the disguise of a hidden covetous intent. The flattering preacher is trying to gain a doorway to your heart in-order to exploit. Nowadays, people are quick to see through such gimmicks and oftentimes this elicits mockery and apathy towards the gospel. When Paul was at Thessalonica, he did not flatter or covet the praise of anyone, neither did he constitute any financial burden to the converts in any way. It sounds so easy except in the doing. For instance, how do you confront a celebrity minister who is preaching an error, especially with a deliberate intent to exploit people? Paul and Silas focused their message completely upon Christ and Salvation. This is important. It is the only thing that changes lives. Some may not get what you preach, but they will certainly imbibe the Spirit of grace where it abounds. Ministers of the gospel shouldn't be focused on their ego or the impression we leave the people of themselves, but rather the testimony they leave of Christ. Our message must point to Christ, away from ourselves.

2.6-9

"Nor of men sought we glory, neither of you, nor yet of others, when we

might have been burdensome, as the apostles of Christ.

⁷ But we were gentle among you, even as a nurse cherishes her children:

⁸ So being affectionately desirous of you, we were willing to have imparted unto you, not the gospel of God only, but also our own souls, because ye were dear unto us.

⁹ For ye remember, brethren, our labor and travail: for laboring night and day, because we would not be chargeable unto any of you, we preached unto you the gospel of God".

Sincere ministers often try to not live off their converts where practicable, or at the least be as moderate as possible in-order not to be financially burdensome to the work of the gospel. Paul and Silas waived their rights to have the Thessalonian Church spend loads of care upon them as Apostles of Christ. The Church had endured so much affliction and in the words of Paul, they tried to treat them like a caring mother would. They worked with their own hands earning wages to support themselves while doing the work of ministry. This is because they were determined to be chargeable to no man for their sustenance in ministry, even though it is not out of place for a minister to be cared for by the Church. Although Paul had a right to take offerings and wages from the Churches he planted, he chose to support himself as a tentmaker, so that he wouldn't add more pressure to the believers. Acts 18:3

2.11-12

"As ye know how we exhorted and comforted and charged every one of you, as a father doth his children,

12 That ye would walk worthy of God, who hath called you unto his kingdom and glory."

No loving father would neglect the safety of his children allowing them to walk into harmful circumstances. He nourished them like a mother, but also warned and charged them like a father to live upright as worthy of their new life in Christ. We must take the new believer under our wings until they mature enough to stand firm in the faith. Then they would have become strong enough to help others too.

2.13

"For this cause also thank we God without ceasing, because, when ye received the word of God which ye heard of us, ye received it not as the

word of men, but as it is in truth, the word of God, which effectually worketh also in you that believe".

This is the only key to profiting from the Word of God. The Thessalonian converts received Paul as God's mouth-piece. His words were oracles of god to them, as if the Lord was speaking directly to them.

How do you view the message of the gospel preached to you? As promises from God and by God, or as the words of a man? Paul is saying here that the reason the Word became effectual in their midst was because of how they received it. Both the preacher and the hearers have a role to play in this. For the Preacher, the word must come:

a. By the Spirit. 1 Cor 2:4
b. Sincere and without guile 2 Cor 1:12, 2:17, 4:5

c. Without jesting Eph. 5:45

d. On the part of the congregation;

e. the Word must be received with holy reverence as oracles of God, and the preacher esteemed highly.1Cor 1:20-25, 1Cor 4:1,14-15;2Cor 3:16.

f. Received with the heart and not just head i.e. not with mere mental assent only. Acts 16:14-15

g. And finally, with readiness to do what is commanded by the word. 2 Cor 8:19, 9:2.

2.14

"For ye, brethren, became followers of the churches of God which in Judaea are in Christ Jesus: for ye also have suffered like things of your own countrymen, even as they have of the Jews:"

Both the Jewish and Gentile brethren suffered persecution each from their own countrymen, but the chief culprits were the zealous religious Jews. They stirred up uproar against the Church and the preaching of the gospel. Acts 13:6-8, Acts 14:2.

Jason in whose house Paul lodged was beaten up, and his whole house ransacked. Others suffered similar fate in their homes and businesses, while others even lost their lives. Persecution is so disheartening especially when it comes from one's own people. Satan barely gives an attention to a believer who stays timid and contained with their faith. But once you step out to preach and testify of the Lord you have to expect opposition. Disapproval and ridicule from your neighbors, peers, fans, and even family. But you should be rest and content with the fact that you will not be the first to suffer for the gospel and no price is too steep to pay for the Testimony of Christ.

2.15-16

"...who both killed the Lord Jesus, and their own prophets, and have persecuted us; and they please not God, and are contrary to all men:

16 Forbidding us to speak to the Gentiles that they might be saved, to fill up their sins all the way: for the wrath is come upon them to the uttermost."

The sins of the Jews included the killing of Jesus Christ when he came to earth as human, and the killing of God's prophets. But now they have stretched it further with the persecution and killing of believers, and forbidding the preaching of Christ to the Gentiles that they too might be saved. When you not only reject the gospel, but constitute yourself an obstacle to the sharing of the gospel to others, Paul describes it as filling up your sins to the uttermost

But why were the Jews so hellbent on stopping the preaching of Christ?

It was purely a selfish self-preservation agenda. The Roman Government had made Judaism legal quite alright, but some officials still had some misgivings with Judaism, especially with Christianity which was viewed as a fanatical and dangerous strand of it. This lumping together detested by the Jewish religious leaders for fear of losing the legal status of Judaism and any possible reprisals that could follow.

Secondly, the Jewish leaders thought Jesus to be a false Prophet. They were also jealous of the rapid spread of the gospel and feared that conversion to Christianity, will weaken their political base and their ability to hold the Roman dominance in check through revolts when and if necessary.

Besides, their prideful status as the only "God's special tribe" came under assault by this new doctrine of the inclusion of Gentiles in the Gospel program.

2.17-20

"But we, brethren, being taken from you for a brief time in presence, not in heart, endeavored the more abundantly to see your face with great desire.

¹⁸ Wherefore we would have come unto you, even I Paul, once and again; but Satan hindered us.

¹⁹ For what is our hope, or joy, or crown of rejoicing? Are not even ye in the presence of our Lord Jesus Christ at his coming?

²⁰ For ye are our glory and joy."

Paul was not one to be pretentious. He openly acknowledged to the Thessalonians that Satan hindered his efforts. He wasn't explicit as to what and how Satan did this. But it could be illness, travel complications, faintheartedness of his colleagues, or any other. Fact is: Satan succeeded in keeping Paul away.

Our take from that is that Satan is real and his determination to oppose the gospel is ever virile. Therefore, ministers of God must be quick to discern these wiles and proactive with the Word of faith in countering him. The Bible calls him the "god of this world". 2Cor 4:4 and "the accuser of the brethren" Rev 12:10. Many of the difficulties we encounter in accomplishing God's call upon our lives are orchestrated by Satan using human beings around us for the most part. There are not enough demons to attach to every person on earth. Yes, there are specific demonic assignments, but most bad is done by men and women who operate under the influence and orientation of the Enemy. Eph 6:12. The aim of Paul's ministry was not money or fame, but the souls of the new converts. That is why he was willing to risk anything to teach and to nourish them. This ought to be our aim too if we are genuinely set out to preach Christ to the world.

CHAPTER - 03

3.1-4

"Wherefore when we could no longer forbear, we thought it good to be left at Athens alone;

²And sent Timotheus, our brother, and minister of God, and our fellowlabourer in the gospel of Christ, to establish you, and to comfort you concerning your faith:

³That no man should be moved by these afflictions: for yourselves know that we are appointed thereunto.

⁴For verily, when we were with you, we told you before that we should suffer tribulation; even as it came to pass, and ye know."

TO THE CHURCH AT THESSALONICA

Sometimes the greatest cares and anxieties facing a minister is the state of his flock. Their welfare and their spiritual health. Are they discouraged and turning back to the world? Are they living their new lives in obedience and joy of the Spirit?

Paul and Silas had such a burden for the Church at Thessalonica. Because of the intense persecution and Paul's in-ability to return there to encourage them, he feared much regarding their welfare.

When trials befall a believer, some are quick to conclude it is a result of sin or lack of faith. This is not usually true. On the contrary, afflictions could be an indication of an effective Christian life. Experiencing problems can build character. Failures and delays help build patience and perseverance.

Rom 5:3-5

³And not only that, but we also glory in tribulations, knowing that tribulation produces perseverance; ⁴and perseverance, character; and character, hope. ⁵Now hope does not disappoint, because the love of God has been poured out in our hearts by the Holy Spirit who was given to us.

The best part of it is that personal tribulation increases our sensitivity towards others who face troubles and misfortune.

In verse 3, Paul makes a very candid statement regarding afflictions as it relates to ministers of the gospel. "We are appointed thereunto". How apt?

Indeed, if you were Satan will you let a man like Paul go unscathed after all he did at Thessalonica? It is the same for every child of God. There's no love lost between Satan and you, and he's not about to let you go just like that. He will try every which way to stop you. Never mind; he can only succeed to make your paths rougher, but the ultimate victory belongs to you already because of Christ's victory on the Cross. It shouldn't be a strange thing for believers when they go through 'stuff'. If you aren't able to do what you want, just do what you can. But, by every means, keep pushing forward and keep trusting in the Lord.

Paul was hindered from returning to Thessalonica, but he sent Timothy to go and inquire of their welfare and bring back a report. Timothy like Paul was willing to risk his life on this mission. Some think that becoming saints of God exempts us from troubles. But God doesn't promise that. Instead He gives us power to grow and mature through afflictions and opposition of the enemy. We must know that even though we are saved, we live and thrive in a world already condemned to decay and degradation. This is a result of Adam's sin.

Rom 5:12:

₁₂ Therefore, just as through one man, sin entered the world, and death through sin, and thus death spread to all men, because all sinned—

Things will progressively get worse until Christ returns to renew the earth. As believers, we are never exempt from the symptoms of the curse of sin and the activities of the un-regenerated men and women working in collusion with Satan. But God's grace is made available and sufficient for us.

2Cor 12:8-9:

⁸ Concerning this thing I pleaded with the Lord three times that it might

depart from me. ⁹And He said to me, "My grace is sufficient for you, for My strength is made perfect in weakness." Therefore, most gladly I will rather boast in my infirmities, that the power of Christ may rest upon me.

3.5 - 8

"⁵For this cause, when I could no longer forbear, I sent to know your faith, lest by some means the tempter have tempted you, and our labor be in vain.

⁶But now when Timotheus came from you unto us, and brought us good tidings of your faith and charity, and that ye have good remembrance of us

always, desiring greatly to see us, as we also to see you:

⁷Therefore, brethren, we were comforted over you in all our affliction and distress by your faith:

⁸For now we live, if ye stand fast in the Lord."

One of the errors taught in the Body of Christ today stems from verse 5 above. Some claim that Paul meant one could lose salvation when you yield to sin. What Paul meant was Satan's effort at uprooting the Church already planted at Thessalonica. It wasn't referring to the salvation of the individual believers. Otherwise we who believe have only believed in vain, since we all at one time or the other yield to the temptation to sin. There's no single believer who is completely free from sinning.

TO THE CHURCH AT THESSALONICA

As expected, Paul, Silas and the brethren at Athens and Berea were overjoyed when Timothy returned with glad tidings about the Thessalonian Church, describing how the disciples there not only stood their ground in the face of fierce persecution, but retained sweet memories of Paul, longing to see him.

It brings extraordinary joy, and every gospel worker knows this feeling, when you see another person come to faith in Christ and overtime mature in their walk in the Lord. Paul enjoyed this feeling so many times and it served as a source of new life and strength to the work. The news from Thessalonica was lifegiving to Paul and his team.

3.9-10

"⁹For what thanks can we render to God again for you, for all the joy

> *wherewith we joy for your sakes before our God;*
>
> *¹⁰Night and day praying exceedingly that we might see your face, and might perfect that which is lacking in your faith?"*

Thanking God for the testimonies meant that Paul and his colleagues acknowledged the source of this success. God made it possible. Sometimes, Apostles and Evangelists tend to be corky after they have become famous and able to attract large following. They soon forget it is the Lord and begin to trust in their charisma and gifts. Some become careless and make fleshly judgements and pursuits. However, because God's gift and calling is without repentance, needs will be met, miracles, healings and crowds will still be there, but the Lord had since been left out of the equation.

3.11

"Now God himself and our Father, and our Lord Jesus Christ, direct our way unto you."

Paul and his colleagues prayed night and day that the Lord will make their return to Thessalonica possible. It is a bit difficult to appreciate this challenge in our day, because of improved means of transportation and communication between cities, countries and even continents of the world. At the time of this epistle, no such facilities existed. Travel was only by sea and prone to weather challenge and other hazards at sea. Besides, Paul had to also contend with the ambush laid for him by the Jews and hostile Gentiles at every stop he made.

For this cause, they sought the face of the Lord continually in prayer. Sometimes the role hardships and delays play in our life and ministry could never be imagined. They mold us into men and women who depend upon the Lord for strength with the result that over time, a young believer matures in his or her walk in Christ.

Gal 5:16:

16 I say then: Walk in the Spirit, and you shall not fulfill the lust of the flesh.

Walking in the Spirit is a learned behavior, just as taking physical steps by a baby is learned. The baby doesn't start out walking confidently. No, it takes measured steps in fear, but overtime learns to walk fast and even run. Afflictions and opposition help to ground us in our spiritual walk. Paul wanted to return to Thessalonica. We have no record that he did, only that when he was travelling through Asia on his 3rd Missionary

Journey, Aristarchus and Secundus who were disciples from Thessalonica joined him.

3.12-13

"₁₂ And the Lord make you to increase and abound in love one toward another, and toward all men, even as we do toward you:

₁₃ To the end he may stablish your hearts unblameable in holiness before God, even our Father, at the coming of our Lord Jesus Christ with all his saints."

Paul prayed for the Thessalonians, that the Lord will make their love grow. Growing in love is the only right and equitable response to God's love which he lavished upon us in Christ. However, this must be a heart growth, not head. In other words, we must increase in love towards others in our hearts, not just in our head. When believers learn godliness like one will learn Physics or Geography, the result is that you succeed in churning out judgmental Christians who resemble Christ only in their words, but not in compassion or character towards the ungodly, and towards even their fellow brethren. They become like the Pharisees of old moving around with a yardstick to measure everyman's compliance to the faith, instead of loving them. Jesus said the only distinguishing mark of a believer is their love for the brethren.

John 13:35

35 By this all will know that you are My disciples, if you have love for one another."

TO THE CHURCH AT THESSALONICA

Paul's prayer for the Thessalonian Church is applicable to all believers everywhere. We receive a full measure of God's love which comes not only through teaching and understanding God's nature, but by stepping out and exercising faith in Him. Only then will the same love flow outwards from us to other people. If you have been in the faith for quite some time and your love dimensions haven't grown, you are probably being fed wrong stuff about God. You are probably ignorant of how much you are loved by Him.

CHAPTER - 04

4.1-8

"Furthermore then we beseech you, brethren, and exhort you by the Lord Jesus, that as ye have received of us how ye ought to walk and to please God, so ye would abound more and more.

² For ye know what commandments we gave you by the Lord Jesus.

³ For this is the will of God, even your sanctification, that ye should abstain from fornication:

⁴ That every one of you should know how to possess his vessel in sanctification and honor;

⁵Not in the lust of concupiscence, even as the Gentiles which know not God:

⁶That no man goes beyond and defraud his brother in any matter: because that the Lord is the avenger of all such, as we also have forewarned you and testified.

⁷For God hath not called us unto uncleanness, but unto holiness.

⁸He therefore that despiseth, despiseth not man, but God, who hath also given unto us his holy Spirit.

The Jews were still under the Law of Moses which had strict injunctions regarding sexual purity. But the Gentiles had no such restrictions or laws. Sexual standards were very low in the Roman Empire. In the modern world of today especially in Western world, they are not any higher. The temptation to indulge sexual behavior outside of marriage has been the bait of Satan as far back as to the ancient, and comes with many hurtful results for individuals, families, careers and even nations. Just as there are physical consequences of sexual promiscuity, there are spiritual implications and dimensions too. Priests of Idol Temples deployed prostitutes to lure male worshippers and hold them spellbound to such religious practices in Bible times. Today, the same is practiced by banks, tourism businesses and their likes.

Besides, sexual perversion has gone one notch up. Homosexuality and lesbianism are fast becoming legal in many countries. Paul warned the Thessalonians not to walk such paths of sexual immorality, stressing that it is the will of God that his children be sanctified, and this sanctification we already have in Christ.

1 Cor 1:30:

"30 But of Him you are in Christ Jesus, who became for us wisdom from God—and righteousness and sanctification and redemption."

Ours is live it out. Sexual desires and activities must be placed under control through yielding our thoughts and bodies to the influence of the HolySpirit and making conscious efforts to be sober, giving dignity to our bodies and not abusing it.

Our holiness does not however derive from what we do or fail to do. We are holy and sanctified by an act of faith, which is receiving Christ and trusting our lives to him. Because Christ is holy and hath exchanged our sinful life for His holiness and righteousness, which exchange we received by faith and not through works. We are sanctified by the washing of water by the Word (Eph.5:26);

and we are cleansed by the Word of the Lord spoken over us (John 15:3), the HolyGhost working with and in us to conform us to the image of Christ. (Rom.8:29).

Paul concludes this admonition of sexual purity by warning that anyone who rejects or refuses to obey this very commandment is not just disobeying a man, he or she is rejecting God who gave his HolySpirit to Paul and the other ministers with him.

4.9-10

"9 But as touching brotherly love ye need not that I write unto you: for ye yourselves are taught of God to love one another.

10 And indeed ye do it toward all the brethren which are in all Macedonia:

but we beseech you, brethren, that ye increase more and more;"

The second area of Paul's emphasis is on "Brotherly love", which Peter also called "Love of the brethren" (1 Peter1:22).It is the very first proof that one has truly embraced the doctrine of Christ. Jesus said: "as I have loved you, so love ye one another'. (John 13:34). This is way different from the Law of Moses which says: "Love thy neighbor as thyself".

The problem with Moses' Law is that many do not love themselves in the first place. The unregenerated man because of the sin-conscience is incapable of loving himself knowing his own secret deeds and being constantly accused by the Enemy. And because you cannot give what you don't have, giving love to another is hardly practicable. But after we have received Christ, the love of God floods our soul and we can freely and superfluously give it to others. The Church of

Thessalonica were already highflyers in this virtue, so much so that it was evident in that whole region of Macedonia. He nudges them on to continue in this virtue.

4.11-12

> *¹¹And that ye study to be quiet, and to do your own business, and to work with your own hands, as we commanded you;*
>
> *¹²That ye may walk honestly toward them that are without, and that ye may have lack of nothing."*

Our duty to the new faith transcends loving just the brethren. Paul here stretches it to those outside of the family of God. How we respond to our neighbors, living and working among them counts. We give testimony of Christ by how we model our daily life to reflect the grace of Christ. The believer should study to be quiet, and mind his own business, giving every dedication to it, Paul admonishes.

The word 'study' is an old English word which connotes a desire or ambition. We are to strive to quieten down on our inside, and to be focused upon our work. That way, we are not only able to provide for ourselves, but also earn the respect of others.

You cannot effectively witness Christ to a man or woman who has no esteem for your person. Some brethren hide under brotherly love to turn themselves into idlers and parasites upon others.

There evidently were a few such misguided fellows in the Thessalonian Church who assumed that the return of the Lord was imminent and hence there was no reason to work or accumulate wealth. Such believers troubled the brethren through peddling of gossip, strife and divisions. Paul warned them to desist, change their ways, find a job, be productive and responsible. This is a timeless admonition which we will do well to receive and uphold in our Churches today. When we do what we do diligently and faithfully we become a positive influence on our society, and a good testimony of the gospel.

Again, the word 'quiet' in this context is a state of mind not an act. Some people look quiet on the outside but inside they have a lot of clamor due to inordinate pursuits and ambition, and a lot of fears, anxieties and strife. A quiet spirit is a virtue learned by daily deploying the fruits of the spirit in our lives.

Gal 5:22:

"₂₂ But the fruit of the Spirit is love, joy, peace, longsuffering, kindness, goodness, faithfulness,

4.13-17

"₁₃ But I would not have you to be ignorant, brethren, concerning them which are asleep, that ye sorrow not, even as others which have no hope.

₁₄ For if we believe that Jesus died and rose again, even so them also which sleep in Jesus will God bring with him.

₁₅ For this we say unto you by the word of the Lord, that we which are alive and remain unto the coming of the Lord shall not prevent them which are asleep. ₁₆ For the Lord himself shall *descend from heaven with a shout, with the voice of the archangel, and with the trump of God: and the dead in Christ shall rise first:*

17 Then we which are alive and remain shall be caught up together with them in the clouds, to meet the Lord in the air: and so, shall we ever be with the Lord.

The question of what happens to those who die in Christ was a burning issue among Thessalonian believers. Many lost their loved ones to the wave of persecution which followed their conversion wondering what will become of those, and what consolations and assurances there is for them.

Paul would not want them to be ignorant about the fate of anyone who dies in Christ.

First, he uses the term 'asleep in the Lord' instead of 'dead', just to emphasize that physical death was not the end of it all. Since Jesus died and broke loose from death and the grave, God will bring back to life all who have slept in the Lord. He affirms to them that he has God's word on this, and that when Christ returns, those of us who are alive in Christ and remain shall not precede those who are already asleep in Him. They shall rise first, and we also following, shall be changed and taken up to meet the Lord in the skies. Yes, we shall fly away to a huge family re-union with the Lord and all saints. An angel of the Lord will blow the trumpet to signal this sometime soon.

4.18

"¹⁸Wherefore comfort one another with these words."

He says to comfort one another, not to scare and unsettle one another, with these words.

This is very worthy of note. Yes, knowing the sequence of events to look out for as preceding 'the Lord's 2nd Coming' is important, but what is more important is knowing the reason why Paul took the time and trouble to detail it. In verse 18 he states it expressly: "therefore, encourage and comfort one another with these words". The purpose is to enjoin believers not to sorrow like people without any hope when their loved one pass. We are assured that it is only temporal, and that we shall be united again. We do not grieve and faint at heart when a brother or sister dies, or even world events take a tragic turn. God will turn our defeats into victories, our tragedies into triumphs, our lack and deprivations into riches, and our pains into glory. For all who sleep in Christ, from Adam to the last of us shall be re-united in glory at the return of the Lord. What could be more reassuring.

TO THE CHURCH AT THESSALONICA

The '2nd Coming' and 'the Rapture' shouldn't be preached in any other way in the Church other than the purpose for which the Holy Ghost intended it, which is cause joy, encourage and inspire hope in the Body of Christ. Any other usage is an abuse.

Some "end-time" prophets (so called) or eschatology experts peddle visions and prophesies which hardly line up with the Bible. They tend to interpret the Word of God in such a way as to cause tumult and despondency, rather than reinforce the hope of salvation. Some even disqualify a cross-section of believers by one reason or the other with claims of visions and revelations of many believers "missing Heaven". This not in line with the truth of Christ's words and his assurances.

John 6:37

"37 All that the Father gives Me will come to Me, and the one who comes to Me I will [a] by no means cast out.

Paul declares most assuredly, that all who sleep in the lord shall rise on that day and be reunited with Him.

CHAPTER - 05

This chapter contains a detailed recount of key events leading up to the 2nd Coming. Two key prophecies will help us here.

Prophet Isaiah describes the 'Day of the Lord' as a day of anger and fierce wrath. A day when even the lights of the heavens shall fail, and so on.

Isaiah 13 vs 9-10:

"Behold, the day of the LORD comes,
Cruel, with both wrath and fierce anger,
To lay the land desolate;
And He will destroy its sinners from it.
10 For the stars of heaven and their

*constellations
Will not give their light;
The sun will be darkened in its going forth,
And the moon will not cause its light to shine."*

Prophet Joel on the other hand captures the dual effect of that cataclysmic event. He predicts it will be a day of judgement for the unbelievers and the reprobates, but also a day of joy, blessing and vindication for the believers in Christ.

Joel 2:30-32

*30 "And I will show wonders in the heavens and in the earth:

Blood and fire and pillars of smoke.
31 The sun shall be turned into*

darkness, and the moon into blood. Before the coming of the great and awesome day of the LORD.³² *And it shall come to pass, that whoever calls on the name of the* LORD *shall be* ⁽ᵃ⁾*saved...*

5.1

"But of the times and the seasons, brethren, ye have no need that I write unto you.

² For yourselves know perfectly that the day of the Lord so cometh as a thief in the night."

The times and seasons which God has set for these events need not be our pre-occupation, neither should it be something we should vigorously exert a discussion on. The reason is obvious. No one knows for sure Paul says, what specific time our Father has programmed these events to occur. Any effort to calibrate the dates or calendar for Christ's return and for the event leading up to it is rather presumptuous, if not foolish. The ,"Y2k of 2000", and "Blood Moons" of 2015, and similar efforts in the past have all come and passed with no significant prediction coming to pass. We are not to allow ourselves to be misled by anyone who claims to know. Our lord himself said that no one knows except the Father.

Mathew 24:36:

"36 "But of that day and hour no one knows, not even the angels of [a]heaven, but My Father only.

What is important is that we are in the beloved; that we are awake and expectant, and that we are rejoicing as the days draw nigh especially as event after event point to His soon return. Alleluia!

5.3

> "3 For when they shall say, Peace and safety; then sudden destruction cometh upon them, as travail upon a woman with child; and they shall not escape."

'When they shall say....'. First, who are the "they"? This is not referring to the believer. Rather it points to the world, the unsaved, and those outside the Body of Christ. The state of the world at the 2nd Coming shall be as it was in the days of Noah. They will wallow in adulation of their human heroes and political leaders who give them false hopes. They will be engrossed in merriment whilst scorning and scoffing at believers who are awaiting the Lord's return. As a result, they will be blindsided by events of the Lord's return. It will come to them like a thief in the night, for while they are busy clinging champagne glasses, a sudden destruction shall swoop upon them.

Could you imagine the kind of celebration that must have been going on in the houses of Jesus's enemies whilst he laid in that tomb? Especially after they had it sealed and secured? To them, it was over. The impostor had been finally nailed. Peace at last. And then, suddenly, on the 3rd day troubling news began to filter in. Their worst fears had become true. Jesus is risen from the dead.

This second coming will be similar. The Angel that spoke to his disciples said: "he will in like manner return to earth". Ours is to be watchful, circumspect and expectant of the glorious hope.

TO THE CHURCH AT THESSALONICA

Hebrews 9:28:

"*²⁸ so Christ was offered once to bear the sins of many. To those who eagerly wait for Him He will appear a second time, apart from sin, for salvation.*

5.9-10

"*⁹ For God hath not appointed us to wrath, but to obtain salvation by our Lord Jesus Christ,*

¹⁰ Who died for us, that, whether we wake or sleep, we should live together with him."

God chose us by himself not unto wrath, but unto salvation. He already exempted the Church from his wrath when he decided to make Jesus bear upon his body the sins of the world and the punishment of death for all men. (Heb. 2:9).

And hence, whether we eat, drink or play, we are united with God through Christ Jesus. We are in him and with him even when he returns to earth. Therefore, we have no fear. Paul admonishes the Church to always encourage, not to tear down people, or scare the living daylights out of them from our pulpits. We are not to exclude those whom the Lord has included in his plan of salvation even when we do not consider them fervent in spirit or as passionately engaged as we expect. To encourage and build-up people is a better 'end-time' ministry than 'scare-mongering' and 'doomsday prophesy' we have everywhere today.

As a long-distance runner, when you near the end of a long marathon, your throat burns, legs wobble, and your heart pants. That's when your friends and fans come in handy to cheer you up and nudge you onto the finish line. This is what believers ought to be to one another in these last days. Paul spent verses 11 - 13 harping on this very important duty and giving specific examples of how we can do just that.

5.11

"Wherefore comfort yourselves together, and edify one another, even as also ye do.

¹²And we beseech you, brethren, to know them which labor among you, and are over you in the Lord, and admonish you;

¹³And to esteem them very highly in love for their work's sake. And be at peace among yourselves".

A good way of encouragement could be to identify and complement whatever roles they play in the Body of Christ, and the admirable qualities they bring to it. We are to honor those who are leaders in the Lord's work. They work hard among us and warn us of all that is wrong. We are to think highly of them and give them sincere love and reverence because of what they do in the gospel, not based upon their social status or age. Leaders in God's work here actually refers to Deacons, Elders, Bishops, and Overseers. Their work in the Lord should be the reason we hold them in high esteem. Their eloquence of speech, beauty or financial standing in society is beside the point. Complement their work and express your appreciation if you have benefitted from their ministry. If you say nothing, how would they know to repeat the good things they do? Complement should be simple, factual and sincere. It must not lead to hero-worship or eye-service which unscrupulous people use to gain undue advantage over leaders.

Paul in verse 13, further advises that we keep on searching for new and improved ways to be more agreeable to others, for even our most difficult contemporaries will be overwhelmed by right attitude and be won back if we show empathy and accept them in love and respect. Place others first and esteem their opinion superior to yours.

5.14

"Now we exhort you, brethren, warn them that are unruly, comfort the feebleminded, support the weak, be patient toward all men".

There are some of our brethren who are weak, but there are those also who are just plain lazy. Paul recommends different approaches to each category.

In the first place, we shouldn't despise or reject them. To the idlers, we are to warn them to change their ways. Sometimes the best ways to do this is to help them with a job.

For the weak, they need support to stand usually with empathy and patience. We are made of different frames, and we have all travelled different routes in life to get to our present. Some were fragile from start, while others got defeated along the way. The key to ministry is the ability to discern between the two, to be sensitive in-order to offer appropriate response and support. You cannot effectively help until you know the problem and you cannot rightly administer the medication if you don't know where the wound is.

5.15-16

"See that none render evil for evil unto any man; but ever follow that which is good, both among

> *yourselves, and to* [16]*Rejoice evermore".*

Rather than requite evil, the Church must learn to absorb pain and receive wrong without the carnal urge to retaliate. This not only refers to the brethren, but also to the outsiders. It's a good measure of maturity in the faith. To rejoice always means to be joyful again and again. Yea, that's who we are called to be.

Joy in the Lord is not the same as happiness. The former is a state of being. It is a fruit of the indwelling presence of God in a person. The latter is only a feeling and is subject to fluctuations. When the unpleasant happens to us, they must not be allowed to obscure what the Lord has already done for us. It must therefore be a conscious decision on our part to stay thankful and joyful in prayer. As we yield to the HolySpirit, we will begin to see how easy staying joyful becomes, and instead of dis-quiet on our inside whenever trouble comes, we will have peace on our inside; the peace of Christ that passeth all understanding.

(Philippians 4:7).

5.17-18

¹⁷Pray without ceasing.

¹⁸In everything give thanks: for this is the will of God in Christ Jesus concerning you."

Instead of being bitter and clamorous we should pray. Prayer is an answer to every challenge we face. We may not be able to spend all our time on our knee but it is possible to maintain a prayerful attitude all the time just by sheer dependence upon the HolySpirit. Simply whispering to the Lord under our breadth in moments of distress as well as in moments of victory is also prayer. This does not set aside in any way, our duty to take out special times to fast and pray neither are we to confuse them both.

Regarding thanksgiving, Paul says we should thank God "in everything'. He didn't say we should thank God "for everything'' that comes our way. That is stupid and unrealistic. Unfortunately, this has become the Creed of most religions of the world. They claim that whatever comes to us whether good or bad is from God. Hurricanes, tsunami, wars and similar calamities are legally classified as "acts of God' which is indeed a mischaracterization of our loving God and Father.

Old testament folks like Job did not have the HolySpirit given unto them as we have today. Therefore, they lacked a true revelation of God, and by extension a poor discernment of Satan. Everything good or bad was ascribed to God.

But we know better.

Evil does not come from God, neither does God deliberately allow evil in-order to teach us some lessons. However, when evil befalls us, God can and does use such circumstances to do good to us any how and any way. So, we are better-off remaining calm and thankful for God's presence in our lives, knowing that when we enter troubled waters, He will work it out for our own good.

Rom 8:28:

28 And we know that all things work together for good to those who love God, to those who are the called according to His purpose "

TO THE CHURCH AT THESSALONICA

5.19-21

> "Quench not the Spirit. [20] Despise not prophesyings. [21] Prove all things; hold fast that which is good."

'Quench not' means do not stifle the work of the Spirit, neither trifle with His work in the lives of others. There are so many ways we fall into this trap. First is when we fail or refuse to cooperate with the HolySpirit when He prompts us to do something good like loving on someone, giving our support to a gospel work, or simply to attend a believer's gathering.

Other ways include maligning a Christian worker thereby wounding their spirit and dampening their zeal in the work of the Lord, despising prophecy, speaking in tongues or other operation of the Spirit amongst God's people.

Sometimes, the exercise of spiritual gifts could become controversial and may cause divisions in Church if not properly handled. Because of this, many Pastors and church leaders err by trying to put a wet blanket over the moves of the Spirit. This shouldn't be, because it impoverishes the Church and makes Christian experience dry and dreary. We shouldn't stifle the work of the HolySpirit in any way, shape or form. This is one area where it is not good to err on the side of caution. We can only test what is spoken, checking it out against the written Word of

God, and adopting only what lines up.

Those who prophesy also have a duty to check and ensure they are prompted by the HolyGhost per time. You needn't have a prophecy for everyone and at every time. That is an abuse of the gift. The Church must prove all things, including prophesy, and hold onto that which is good.

TO THE CHURCH AT THESSALONICA

5.22

"Abstain from all appearance of evil."

Believers must make it a deliberate policy to keep away from evil. This includes both evil company, evil thoughts and an evil conscience. Sometimes what we read in books or watch on television are not in our best interest, as Satan gains an entrance into our innermost recesses through such a medium. For the World Media, only bad is newsworthy. When someone predicts that the economy will crash in 3 months, it's newsworthy. When a plane crashes in one country killing all onboard, it's newsworthy. When mad-cow disease breaks out in one country and someone predicts that nearly three quarters of all cattle globally will die, that's newsworthy. All these create fear and instability in your mind.

Aside the media, there are also people around us whose opinion we hold in high esteem. Some of them give evil counsel and discouragement. That is one cheap source of evil tidings we should avoid. This doesn't say that we should lock-up ourselves in the room, or un-friend every acquaintance we already have, but we are to place Christ and our knowledge of Him in-between us and such influences, so that they come through Christ before getting at us. Make no mistakes about it; "evil communication corrupts good manners". (1 Cor 15:33).

5.23

"And the very God of peace sanctify you wholly; and I pray God your whole spirit and soul and body be preserved blameless unto the coming of our Lord Jesus Christ."

TO THE CHURCH AT THESSALONICA

Sanctification is a separation for holy use. As you yield yourself to the HolySpirit, you are continually consecrated and set aside for holy use by God. In this way, sanctification is a progressive experience, but holiness is not. We are not holy by ourselves, but our holiness is "in Him". It's a product of our justification by the shed blood of Christ and his resurrection from the dead. At the point of the "New Birth", we have been made as holy as Christ. (Rom 8:9,1 John 4:17). And we have become one with him. (1 Cor 6:17). He is also not ashamed to call us his brothers and sisters because we are one with him. (Heb. 2:11).

Holiness is a gift we receive along with receiving Christ into our hearts, and we become instantly as holy as we could ever be, but that is in our spirit man only. The mind and body begin a process of renewal as we walk with the Lord. Our sanctification grows as we come to the knowledge of God's will and progressively yield to the influence of the HolyGhost in our lives. As sanctification grows, obedience becomes easier. (Gal 5:16, Col 2:6).

It's noteworthy that Paul in verse 23 categorized the human person into three components, namely: the "spirit", the "soul" and the "body". Our spirit is that part of us that becomes renewed and made into Christ's righteousness at new birth. Our soul is our mind and intellect. This is the center of our thoughts, emotion, character and will. It must be turned away from the flesh and progressively renewed by the word of God through teaching and fellowship of the saints. Our body is the physical earth suit required by all spirits including our good selves to operate here on earth. Christ himself had to also take up a body to live on earth as a man. Our body is unruly, carnal and compromised by sinful desires. Contrary to what many of us think, the body is not only in opposition to the born-again spirit in us, but it is in enmity with God.

Rom 8:7:

"7 Because the [a]carnal mind is enmity against God; for it is not subject to the law of God, nor indeed can be".

But we have a guarantee from God that the process of quickening of our bodies had begun at new birth and will culminate into the transformation which will happen at the Rapture. (Rom 8:11).

In the light of the above, we shouldn't be too quick to judge a believer, or deny them fellowship based on their present habits which we may consider sinful or un-becoming.

Nonetheless, the true measure of the progress made by us or by others in the walk with the Lord is how we behave and carry on our normal daily lives. The prayer of verse 23 is simply Paul affirming that God needs to become part of all the aspects of our being, not just our spirit only.

5.27

"²⁷I charge you by the Lord that this epistle be read unto all the holy brethren."

Paul commanded the Thessalonian Church to extend the message of this epistle to all other Churches within their region. The gospel should not be restrained by denominational walls. So much progress could be made if believing congregations could see themselves as one and share things with one another. For all Christians to share this letter was a great idea, and you could see how that gesture continues today. Paul's epistle is read and taught in all Churches, but the revelation content varies from one Church to another.

Part - Two

This is a follow-up to the first epistle to the Thessalonians by Paul.

In this epistle, Paul details his predictions of the events leading up to the 2nd Coming. Already there was a growing misconception of the things Paul said in the first epistle. Even when written down, words oftentimes do get misconstrued especially when sieved through our own prejudices and beliefs. The 1st epistle was Paul simply trying to encourage and mature the Church, but some seized it for an excuse to stop working and earning support for their families, pointing to the imminent return of the Lord. In view of the fierce persecution that befell them, it seemed very logical to give up working and even other daily routines of life and be solely pre-occupied with this blissful hope of the Rapture as an escape from all their troubles. Paul had to quickly write this second epistle in-order to dispel the rumors, and clarify issues raised by his earlier epistle.

Even though the '2nd Coming' is a certain and factual event to occur on the earth, there has been a lot of confusion about the timings due to wrong teachings, in the early Church, and even in today's Church. It is now almost two thousand years after this epistle was written. The Church stands yet much closer to the time of Christ's return, but no one can pin-point or say with exactitude the very timing of it. It is foolhardy to resort to idle speculating and 'star-gazing' about it, instead of engaging on our work and the spreading of the gospel which we have been called to. Expectation of Christ's return should be our watchword, and our occupation. We are to engage the lost world as never before through evangelism, while at the same time teaching and edifying the present Church, the only pillar and ground of truth.

CHAPTER - 01

1.1-7

"Paul, and Silvanus, and Timotheus, unto the church of the Thessalonians in God our Father and the Lord Jesus Christ:

²Grace unto you, and peace, from God our Father and the Lord Jesus Christ.

³We are bound to thank God always for you, brethren, as it is meet, because that your faith groweth exceedingly, and the charity of every one of you all toward each other aboundeth;

⁴So that we ourselves glory in you in the churches of God for your patience

and faith in all your persecutions and tribulations that ye endure:

5 Which is a manifest token of the righteous judgment of God, that ye may be counted worthy of the kingdom of God, for which ye also suffer:

6 Seeing it is a righteous thing with God to recompense tribulation to them that trouble you;

7 And to you who are troubled rest with us, when the Lord Jesus shall be revealed from heaven with his mighty angels,

The news reaching Paul from Thessalonica was a mixture of the 'Good, the Bad and the Ugly'. The good news: 'the Church was still in place and thriving'.

The bad: that the persecution of the Church by both Jews and Gentile Greeks persisted and even intensified.

But the ugly, which perturbed Paul most was that some religious impostor appended a forged signature of Paul to a letter bearing certain false doctrines, using it to cause confusion and panic regarding the Lord's return.

Paul opened this epistle by acknowledging God for the good news and acknowledging the Church for their positive response to the gospel, stating how personally elated he was as a result. The most important duty of a minister is to encourage and to affirm the brethren, and not to tear them down with criticism. All are to emulate Paul on this.

1.8-10

"⁸In flaming fire taking vengeance on them that know not God, and that

> *obey not the gospel of our Lord Jesus Christ:*
>
> *⁹Who shall be punished with everlasting destruction from the presence of the Lord, and from the glory of his power;*
>
> *¹⁰When he shall come to be glorified in his saints, and to be admired in all them that believe (because our testimony among you was believed) in that day."*

There is a reward he says, for those who endure persecution to the end. God will not only make it good for us but will also vindicate us by righteously avenging our oppressors. Part of this reward is the 'rest with us' statement in verse 7.

The Church is at rest now, even amidst these attacks and trials, but this rest shall be fully consummated on the Lord's day when Christ is revealed from heaven to take vengeance on the traducers of the Church and all mockers and scoffers of this world. This hope ought to be a stabilizing factor for believers of all time. Paul had been persecuted during his trip to Thessalonica, so he knew firsthand what the brethren there were up against. To date, the persecution of Christians for their faith hasn't abated even with all the advances recorded by civilization. Rather, it is expected to be on the progressive rise as we approach the end of the age. Paul therefore warns the church to gird up their loins and embrace their fate with courage and patience resting on the hope of a certain future event called the "Lord's day'. As we live for Christ, we will experience troubles because we are trying to be God's people in a perverse world. This isn't out of place but rather lines up with the words of our Lord Himself.

John 15:18-19:

¹⁸ "If the world hates you, you know that it hated Me before it hated you. ¹⁹ If you were of the world, the world would love its own. Yet because you are not of the world, but I chose you out of the world, therefore the world hates you.

Both Paul and Peter agree that troubles are the trials of our faith rather than a result of sin or punishment for our personal shortcomings. Troubles could indeed be a positive force to get us to look upward in dependence upon the Lord. Besides, when we overcome our own afflictions, it equips us to comfort and help others who are facing same.

2Cor 1:3-5:

³ Blessed be the God and Father of our Lord Jesus Christ, the Father of mercies and God of all comfort, ⁴ who comforts us in all our tribulation, that we may be able to comfort those who are in any trouble, with the comfort with which we ourselves are comforted by God. ⁵ For as the sufferings of Christ abound in us, so our consolation also abounds through Christ.

The relief of the suffering believer is two-fold. First is knowing that God is in it with us, strengthening and building our character and faith. Secondly, we can also gain relief in the fact that one day, we shall all stand before God, where all wrongs shall be righted, judgement pronounced on the ungodly, and evil terminated forever. What a solace and vindication it shall be. We need not be anxious about when all these are going to happen. Ours is to be rested in the Word of the Lord, looking up expectantly in all confidence to that day, knowing that we already have an anchor within the veil, our Christ Jesus. Heb 6:19

1.11-12

"11 Wherefore also we pray always for you, that our God would count you worthy of this calling, and fulfil all the good pleasure of his goodness, and the work of faith with power: 12 That the name of our Lord Jesus Christ may be glorified in you, and ye in him, according to the grace of our God and the Lord Jesus Christ."

Our calling is to become part of God through and through. To be joined unto Him by reason of adoption as sons conforming to the image of Christ who is the prototype of the 'New Man". (Rom 8:29, Eph. 2:10). The body although now in progressive decay, shall not be completely lost. If we die, the body is buried into the ground and becomes dust. But only temporarily. At the Rapture, all in Christ, both the dead and the living shall receive brand new immortal bodies. We have an assurance on this. When Jesus rose from the dead, he took up his body again, but this time a glorified body, and so shall we, Paul assures.

Paul's prayer that the Lord will consider them worthy of his calling doesn't mean they were short, or that they needed to qualify or earn God's acceptance. No, that would mean that Christ's mission is somewhat un-finished, and his justification incomplete. Rather, to be worthy of his calling means that God will make them fit for what he had called each of them to become, God filling them with ideas and promptings to fulfill his purpose in their lives.

Yielding to God, the work we accomplish thereby shall in turn bring glory and testimony to His grace.

CHAPTER - 02

2.1-5

"Now we beseech you, brethren, by the coming of our Lord Jesus Christ, and by our gathering together unto him,

²That ye be not soon shaken in mind, or be troubled, neither by spirit, nor by word, nor by letter as from us, as that the day of Christ is at hand.

³Let no man deceive you by any means: for that day shall not come, except there come a falling away first, and that man of sin be revealed, the son of perdition;

⁴Who opposeth and exalteth himself above all that is called God, or that is worshipped; so that he as God sitteth

> *in the temple of God, shewing himself that he is God.*
>
> *⁵ Remember ye not, that, when I was yet with you, I told you these things?*

When you use the word beseech on a matter, it is a passionate appeal. Paul was entreating the Thessalonians in the name of the Lord to consider his appeal in the light of two cardinal points of our faith: The coming of the Lord; and our fellowship with one another. These two are the chief creed of our faith.

The 2nd Coming of Christ is a certain event which shall soon come to pass on earth. The challenge is not that the Thessalonians didn't believe it, but rather that they swung from one extreme to the other on it. When Paul wrote his first epistle it was because they were at the very edge of disbelieving it. Then after reading that epistle, they swung to the opposite extreme by believing that the event was at the door and hence their resignation from their jobs and routine activities. Paul's mission in this second epistle was to bring balance to this teaching.

He invokes 'our fellowship' or gathering together, as the second grounds of his appeal. The significance of our fellowship together can never be overemphasized. Paul admonishes every believer to endeavor to keep the unity of the Spirit. (Eph.4:3).

Nothing best guarantees this than the gathering of saints together to worship.

Regarding the 2nd coming and the end of the world, Paul warns in verse 3, that great suffering and evil lie ahead, but that evil will not triumph over good, because of what Christ will do. Some false teachers were saying to the Thessalonian Church that the "Judgment day" has already begun and by so doing, took advantage of many gullible folks who already were desperate for relief from persecution and suffering in any way, shape or form. Paul's position on this was not a mere suggestion. He authoritatively declared that the judgment day had not yet come. There are certain events which must precede it, he says. Therefore, let the Thessalonian Church or any other be warned to disregard any vision or letter purportedly sent by him on this matter.

Obviously, some false brother was claiming to have had a divine revelation on the end time events, (as many do today to their own shame), and the worst part, he was dropping Paul's name to authenticate himself. Paul out-rightly dissociated himself from this guy. Quacks like him are never in short supply in today's Church. Time and again, Believers, even the finest of them fall prey to this error.

The "Man of Sin" or "Man of Lawlessness" of scriptures shall be revealed before the 2nd Coming. He will be a complete God-defying and beastly personality who will rise to popularity on earth and whose influence shall extend rapidly around the globe through sheer deceit. He will be Satan's attack dog and shall be enabled to perform signs and wonders to deceive all those who have rejected the love of God and knowledge of the truth. At the time of Paul's prediction, the rise of the Anti-Christ and the rapid spread of his influence around the globe would seem somewhat improbable, but with the discovery of the internet and global satellite media, it becomes clear how this is very feasible. These developments are also indicators of his imminent appearance on the scene.

However, it is an error and spiritual dumbness to label anyone "the Anti-Christ", be it the Pope, Russian or American Leader as many wide-eyed speculators do today. Mention of the Anti-Christ is not a clarion call to the Church to shoot off in that direction trying to identify or pin-point which geographical location he will emanate from. No. The purpose is simply that the Church be warned to stay firm through to the end. He reminds them

TO THE CHURCH AT THESSALONICA

again of his earlier warnings on this subject whilst he was at Thessalonica.

2.6-8

> "And now ye know what withholdeth that he might be revealed in his time. 7 For the mystery of iniquity doth already work: only he who now letteth will let, until he be taken out of the way.
>
> 8 And then shall that Wicked be revealed, whom the Lord shall consume with the spirit of his mouth and shall destroy with the brightness of his coming."

Here Paul reminded the Church that they already know what is hindering the Anti-Christ from showing up. They already know, means that he taught them.

It should be the wish and pre-occupation of every minister that his Church be thoroughly knowledgeable in the New testament. If the Thessalonian Church of 54 AD already knew so much about the Anti-Christ and the sequence of events leading up to the 2nd Coming, why then is there so much ignorance today about it? Why can't the Church see that lawlessness is building up openly already and the underground preparations for the coming world government is afoot. Even Western civilization, with their firm grip on law and order, will be seeing a complete and total breakout of anarchy in the very near future. This Paul states will only happen when the "He" of 2 Thessalonians 2:7 has been taken out of the way. In other words, the secret power is already working in the world now, but there is one who is stopping that secret power from full operation and "He" will continue to do so until the day comes when God takes him out of the way.

Who is the "He" Paul refers to in this verse?

TO THE CHURCH AT THESSALONICA

First, it is something or someone already known, who hinders the Anti-Christ from full manifestation, and will continue to hinder lawlessness until he (or it) is removed from the earth and therefore, shall not be present when Christ destroys the Anti-Christ. Although Paul never stated expressly who this 'hinderer of lawlessness' is, the soundest of Bible scholars favor the Church to be the 'he'. The Governments of the world couldn't be it because they are all in a cascading fall presently and will fall cheaply to the anti-Christ.

It also couldn't be the HolySpirit because Jesus said the HolySpirit shall dwell in the earth forever, and as long as there is one believer on earth, the HolySpirit will be here.

John 14:16:

16 And I will pray the Father, and He will give you another [a]Helper, that He may abide with you forever–

By process of elimination, that leaves us with the Church as the only possible single factor hindering the manifestation of the Man of Lawlessness and the only one who aptly fits Paul's descriptions.

The Church will only be removed from the earth by a future event known as the Rapture. (1 Thess 4;16). In the interim, we shall continue to hinder lawlessness through prayer and the spreading the gospel.

2.9

"⁹ Even him, whose coming is after the working of Satan with all power and signs and lying wonders,"

What will the Man of Sin do? This evil personality, the Anti-Christ will use counterfeit powers of signs and wonder to deceive and draw a great followership. A miracle is a veritable tool for advancing the gospel and strengthening the faith of believers. But not every miracle is from God. Worse still, that a man works a miracle doesn't mean he knows the mind of God on all things. He too could be deceived at any point if he fails to be discerning enough. The Church is to be led by men and women who know the Word of God and are in tune with the HolySpirit. Ability to work miracle is not proof of that. For the gift and calling of God is without repentance. (Rom 11:29). Even when a miracle worker is ignorant of or out of tune with God's program, the miraculous will still operate in his life.

2.10-12

"₁₀ And with all deceivableness of unrighteousness in them that perish; because they received not the love of the truth, that they might be saved.

₁₁ And for this cause, God shall send them strong delusion, that they should believe a lie:

₁₂ That they all might be damned who believed not the truth but had pleasure in unrighteousness."

Men perish for only one reason. Not because they sinned, but because the failed to receive the truth of God's love and salvation. God doesn't force anyone to come under his will, even though he wills for all men to be saved. Those who hear the gospel and reject it will have an active accomplice and enabler in the anti-Christ. Together with him, they will also receive the recompense of their willful rejection of the Spirit of grace. Paul consistently taught that salvation begins and ends with God. He reminds us that we were chosen from the beginning by God and can look up to him alone for sustenance along the road we now travel. We are to stand fast in the injunctions and well laid out doctrines of the gospel.

CHAPTER - 03

3.1-3

"Finally, brethren, pray for us, that the word of the Lord may have free course, and be glorified, even as it is with you:

²And that we may be delivered from unreasonable and wicked men: for all men have not faith.

But the Lord is faithful, who shall stablish you, and keep you from evil."

The threat of spiritual attack should not be taken lightly. Paul never did, but instead sought prayers from the brethren to counter all the assaults of the enemy upon them and their mission. Among the

TO THE CHURCH AT THESSALONICA

New Testament writers, only Paul is recorded to have asked for prayers from his converts. (see Rom 15:30, 2 Cor 1:11). His prayer is worthy of note also; first, that the gospel may have free course, meaning to flow unhindered by Satanic attack. Oftentimes, as soon as we set out on a noble gospel project, all hell is let loose to hinder it and dampen our spirit if possible. We must recognize it as the work of the enemy.

Secondly that the Word of God be glorified. The evidence of this is when men are saved and become obedient to the faith. (Acts 6:7)

Thirdly, for protection of himself and his team, and indeed all gospel preachers from discouragement.

Oftentimes, burn-out, offense, financial lack, marital problems, sickness and personal injury, as well as death are very common tools deployed by the Enemy to antagonize the gospel. In all these, our only weapon or defense is prayer and our clinging unto the Lord steadfastly in hope.

3.4-5 "⁴ And we have confidence in the Lord touching you, that ye both do and will do the things which we command you.

⁵ And the Lord direct your hearts into the love of God, and into the patient waiting for Christ."

Confidence is a two-way traffic. Faithfulness on God's part, and complete trust from us. The Lord's part is the constant in this equation. Paul here expresses his confidence in the Lord that He will keep him from evil and establish his good purposes. He also prayed for the brethren that they will be obedient to the faith, adhering to his admonition. There's no better way to demonstrate our conversion than in submission to instructions of ministers whom the Lord has placed over us.

TO THE CHURCH AT THESSALONICA

3.6-10

"⁶ Now we command you, brethren, in the name of our Lord Jesus Christ, that ye withdraw yourselves from every brother that walketh disorderly, and not after the tradition which he received of us. ⁷ For yourselves know how ye ought to follow us: for we behaved not ourselves disorderly among you;

⁸ Neither did we eat any man's bread for nought; but wrought with labour and travail night and day, that we might not be chargeable to any of you:

⁹ Not because we have not power, but to make ourselves an ensample unto you to follow us.

> ¹⁰ *For even when we were with you, this we commanded you, that if any would not work, neither should he eat.*
>
> ¹¹ *For we hear that there are some which walk among you disorderly, working not at all, but are busybodies.*
>
> ¹² *Now them that are such we command and exhort by our Lord Jesus Christ, that with quietness they work, and eat their own bread."*

He follows up with fresh instructions regarding those who walk dis-orderly, thereby sending out wrong and confusing signals about the Church and the new life in Christ. Some slacked from work choosing to become parasites on other brethren. Others became 'idle-talkers' peddling rumors and gossips which cause divisions in the Church. Paul commanded the Church to withdraw from such people, stating that whosoever does not work should not eat. Believers ought to make the most use of their talents and opportunities to provide not only their own needs, but also the needs of others.

Nevertheless, supporting the weak and sharing our blessings with others is still an all-time Christian virtue necessary for a healthy church community. Believers should not use Paul's admonition as an excuse to shut their bowels of mercy or become weary in well-doing, neither should indolence be confused for spirituality. Those who insist on such poor attitudes are to be shamed.

Maranatha!

www.ingramcontent.com/pod-product-compliance
Lightning Source LLC
Chambersburg PA
CBHW070458100426
42743CB00010B/1670